WORDSWORTH ART PRINTS

The Portfolio Book

of

MARINE ART

MARINE ART

Marine art is a particular form of landscape painting, and it is often difficult to differentiate between the two. They both became popular subjects for artists at virtually the same time. Marine artists depict calm or stormy seas and coastlines, usually with the addition of ships, typical subjects also including beach and harbour views, naval battles, historical pictures and fishing scenes. Early examples of marine art, contained within depictions of biblical or mythological subjects, are to be found in Greek vase paintings and the wall paintings of Pompeii, but the earliest specific seascape appears to be *Storm at Sea* by Pieter Bruegel the Elder. The *genre* reached the peak of its development in the 17th century, when the merchant shipping and naval power of the northern provinces of the Netherlands were at their height. Marine artists concentrated initially on the portrayal of ships and the depiction of historical events, which were rendered with documentary accuracy and in glowing natural colours. It was not until the interplay of light and shade became a central concern in Dutch marine art that depictions of the poetry of northern seascapes became increasingly important. Jan Porcellis was the first to portray water as a subject in its own right, and it was his work that provided the essential impetus for the further development of the *genre*. Landscape motifs, stretches of water, vast expanses of sky extending high above a low horizon and greyish-blue gradations of tone unifying the whole composition all contribute to the overall impression of his paintings. His work influenced Jan van Goyen, Simon de Vlieger, Jan van de Capelle and Willem van de Velde the Younger, and they succeeded wonderfully in conveying the atmosphere of light and air over shimmering water. The emphasis on more brilliant colouring that was favoured after the turn of the century further heightened the atmospheric rendering of the play of light, air and water and made for even more striking compositions. At the same time, Claude Lorrain was producing his southern harbour scenes in Italy, to be followed in the 18th century by the Frenchman Claude Joseph Vernet, who specialised in dramatic images of storms and distress at sea that were intended as allegories of the human condition. In Venice, Francesco Guardi in particular cultivated the tradition of seascape painting. Marine art went through a period of revival in the 19th century, when the pure seascape without the addition of ships and human figures emerged. The works of John Constable and William Turner opened up new means of expression, while the German Romantics, and particularly the heavily symbolic paintings of Caspar David Friedrich, offered a new interpretation of the *genre*. Many American painters of the 19th century, such as Winslow Homer, John Friedrich Knesset and Fritz Hugh Lane, also included seascapes in their output. Finally, the pointillists Georges Seurat and Paul Signac, the Fauvists Raoul Dufy and Albert Marquet and the expressionists Emil Nolde and, in particular, Lyonel Feininger all enriched the *genre* in their own distinctive ways.

Michael Ancher, 1849-1927
The Lifeboat is Carried Through the Dunes, 1883
Oil on canvas, 171 x 221 cm
Copenhagen, Statens Museum for Kunst

Ludolf Backhuysen, 1631-1708
The IJ at Amsterdam, 1673
Oil on canvas, 81 x 67 cm
Amsterdam, Rijksmuseum

Johannes Bosboom, 1817-1891
The Beach at Scheveningen, c.1873
Aquarelle, 35 x 55 cm
Amsterdam, Rijksmuseum

Henri-Edmond Cross, 1856-1910
The Isles of Gold, 1892
Oil on canvas, 59 x 54 cm
Paris, Musée d'Orsay

Gustave Courbet, 1819-1877
The Cliff of Étretat after the Storm, 1869
Oil on canvas, 133 x 162 cm
Paris, Musée National de Louvre

Gustave Courbet, 1819-1877
Lake Léman at Sunset, c.1876
Oil on canvas, 74 x 100 cm
St. Gall, Kunstmuseum

John Constable, 1776-1837
Weymouth Bay, 1816
Oil on board, 50,4 x 62,5 cm
London, Victoria and Albert Museum

Jan van de Capelle, 1626-1679
A Dutch Yacht Firing a Salute, 1650
Oil on canvas, 85,5 x 114,5 cm
London, The National Gallery

Canaletto, 1697-1768
Venice: La Punta della Dogana, c.1726/30
Oil on canvas, 46 x 63,4 cm
Vienna, Kunsthistorisches Museum

Raoul Dufy, 1877-1953
The Pier of Honfleur, 1930
Oil on canvas, 46 x 56 cm
Saint-Tropez, Musée de l'Annonciade

Christoffer Wilhelm Eckersberg, 1783-1853
The Russian Line-of-battle-ship "Asow", 1828
Oil on canvas, 63 x 51 cm
Copenhagen, Statens Museum for Kunst

Lyonel Feiniger, 1871-1956
Sidewheeler, 1913
Oil on canvas, 81 x 100,5 cm
Detroit, The Detroit Institute of Arts

Caspar David Friedrich, 1774-1840
Moon-rise over the Sea, 1822
Oil on canvas, 55 x 71 cm
Berlin, Staatliche Museen

Paul Gaugin, 1848-1903
Rocks in the Sea, 1886
Oil on canvas, 71 x 92 cm
Gothenburg, Konstmuseum

Théodore Géricault, 1791-1824
The Raft of the Medusa, 1818
Oil on canvas, 65 x 83 cm
Paris, Musée National de Louvre

Vincent van Gogh, 1853-1890
The Sea at Saintes-Maries, 1888
Oil on canvas, 44 x 53 cm
Moscow, Pushkin Museum of Fine Arts

Jan van Goyen, 1596-1656
The Haarlemmer Lake, 1656
Oil on canvas, 40 x 69 cm
Frankfort, Städelsches Kunstinstitut

Winslow Homer, 1836-1910
Northeaster, 1895
Oil on canvas,
New York, The Metropolitan Museum of Art
Gift of George A. Hearn

Christian Krogh, 1852-1925
Leif Erikson discovers America, 1893
Oil on canvas, 313 x 470 cm
Oslo, Nasjonalgalleriet

Peder Severin Krøyer, 1851-1909
Summer-evening at Skagen,
The Artists Wife with a Dog on the Beach, 1892
Oil on canvas, 206 x 123 cm
Skagen, Skagens Museum

Fitz Hugh Lane, 1804-1865
New York Harbour, 1850
Oil on canvas
Boston (Mass), Museum of Fine Arts

Claude Lorrain, 1600-1682
Odysseus Restoring Chryseis to Her Father, 1647
Oil on canvas, 119 x 150 cm
Paris, Musée National du Louvre

Édouard Manet, 1832-1883
The Escape of Rochefort, 1880
Oil on canvas, 80 x 73 cm
Private Collection

Jacob Maris, 1837-1899
The Bluff-bowed Fishing-boat, 1878
Oil on canvas, 124 x 105 cm
The Hague, Haags Gemeentemuseum

Anton Melbye, 1818-1875
The Lighthouse of Eddystone, 1861
Oil on canvas, 92 x 143 cm
Private Collection

Hendrik Willem Mesdag, 1831-1915
Fishing Boats in the Breakers
Aquarelle, 48 x 63,5 cm
Amsterdam, Rijksmuseum

Claude Monet, 1840-1926
The Rocks of Belle-Ile, 1886
Oil on canvas, 65 x 81 cm
Moscow, Pushkin Museum of Fine Arts

Theo van Rysselberghe, 1862-1926
Sailing Boats on an Estuary, c.1892/93
Oil on canvas, 50 x 61 cm
Paris, Musée d'Orsay

Georges Seurat, 1859-1891
Port-en-Bessin, Outer Harbour, High Tide, 1888
Oil on canvas, 61 x 82 cm
Paris, Musée d'Orsay

Charles Sheeler, 1883-1965
Pertaining to Yachts and Yachting, 1922
Oil on canvas, 40,8 x 61 cm
Philadelphia, Museum of Art

Paul Signac, 1863-1935
The St-Jean Fort, Marseilles, 1907
Oil on canvas, 50 x 61 cm
Saint-Tropez, Musée de l'Annonciade

Abraham Storck, 1635-1710
A Sham Fight on the IJ at Amsterdam
on September 1697. Oil on canvas, 50 x 66 cm
Amsterdam Historisch Museum

Joseph Mallord William Turner, 1775-1851
The Battle of Trafalgar, c.1806/08
Oil on canvas, 171 x 238,5 cm
London, The Tate Gallery

Joseph Mallord William Turner, 1775-1851
Rockets and Blue Lights (close at hand)
to Warn Steam-boats of Shoal Water, 1840
Oil on canvas, 91,8 x 122,2 cm
Williamstown (Mass.),
Sterling and Francine Clark Art Institute

Joseph Mallord William Turner, 1775-1851
Fishermen on a Lee-shore, 1802
91,5 x 122 cm
London, Kenwood, The Iveagh Bequest

Adriaen van de Velde, 1636-1672
The Beach at Scheveningen, 1658
Oil on canvas, 50 x 74 cm
Kassel, Staatliche Kunstsammlungen

Willem van de Velde, 1633-1707
The Cannon Shot
Oil on canvas, 78,4 x 67 cm
Amsterdam, Rijksmuseum

Willem van de Velde, 1633-1707
The Gust of Wind, c.1670
Oil on canvas, 77 x 63,5 cm
Amsterdam, Rijksmuseum

Willem van de Velde, 1633-1707
The IJ at Amsterdam, 1686
Oil on canvas, 179,5 x 316 cm
Amsterdam, Rijksmuseum

Jens Ferdinand Willumsen, 1863-1958
After the Storm, 1905
Oil on canvas, 155 x 150 cm
Oslo, Nasjonalgalleriet

How to Use this Book

Thirty-nine of the forty prints in this book are easily removed. Open the book and press it onto a flat surface, and grip the desired print firmly with the other hand. Pull it diagonally from the binding and it will come away leaving a clean edge. It is now ready for framing. The first print in the book may be cut away with a scalpel or knife. Alternatively, you may wish to keep the book intact as a valuable reference source.

The prints are suitable for framing using ready-made framing kits, available from framing, print and poster shops. The simplest of these kits are the clip-style frames which consist of a backing board, a sheet of backing paper (usually white with a black verso), a perspex or glass front and clips to hold the frame together. You can buy wooden frames complete with cut-out mount. There is a very large range of styles and prices for ready-made frames.

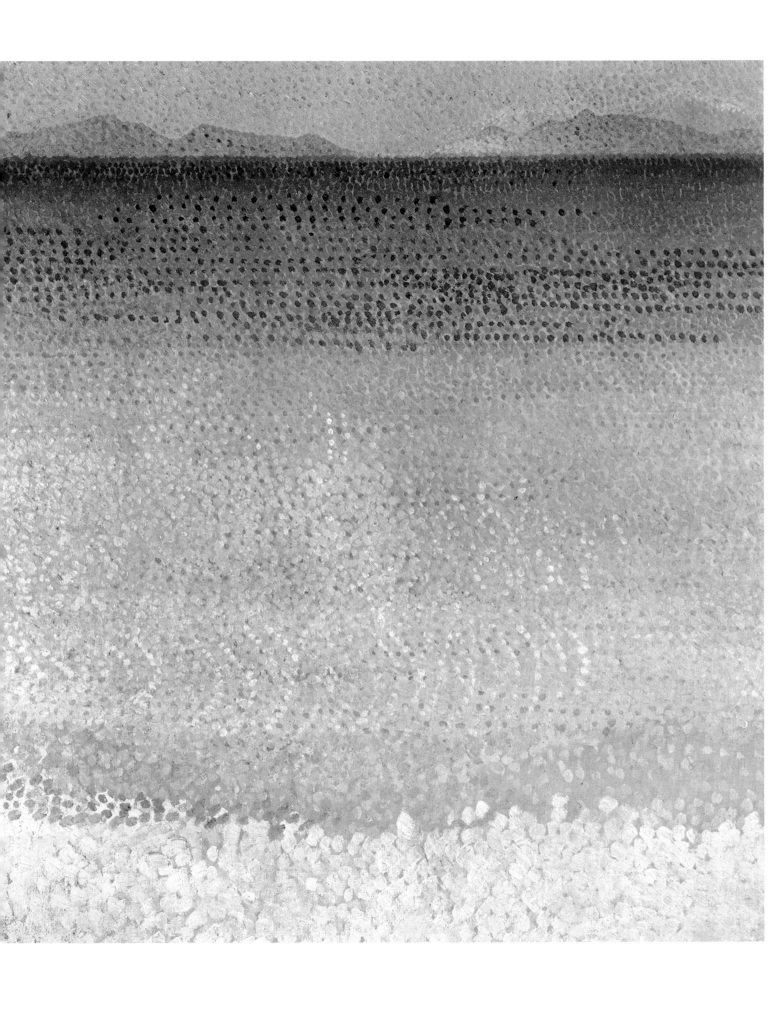

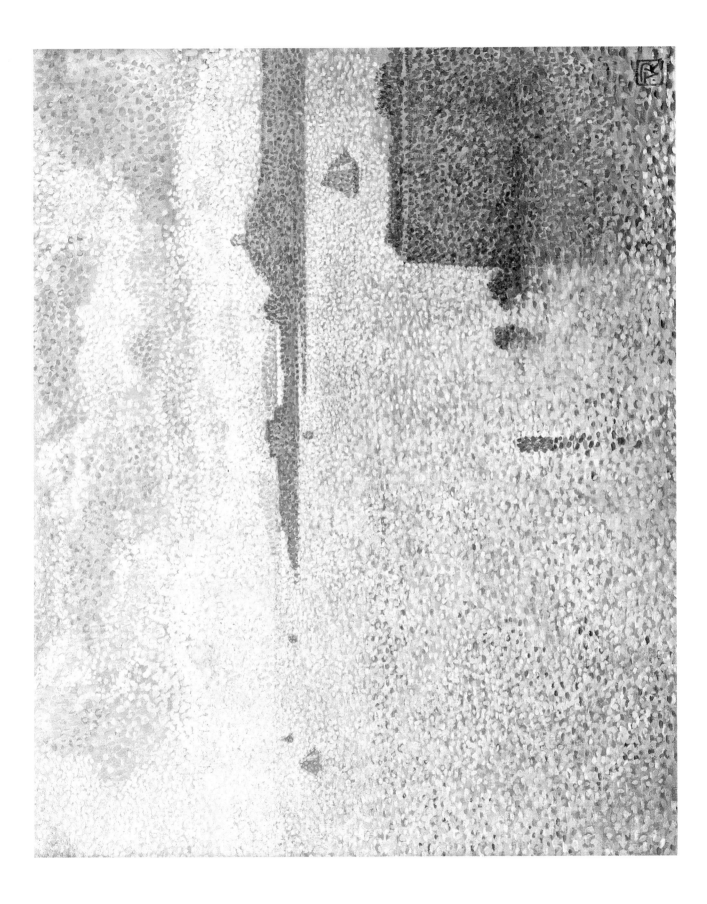

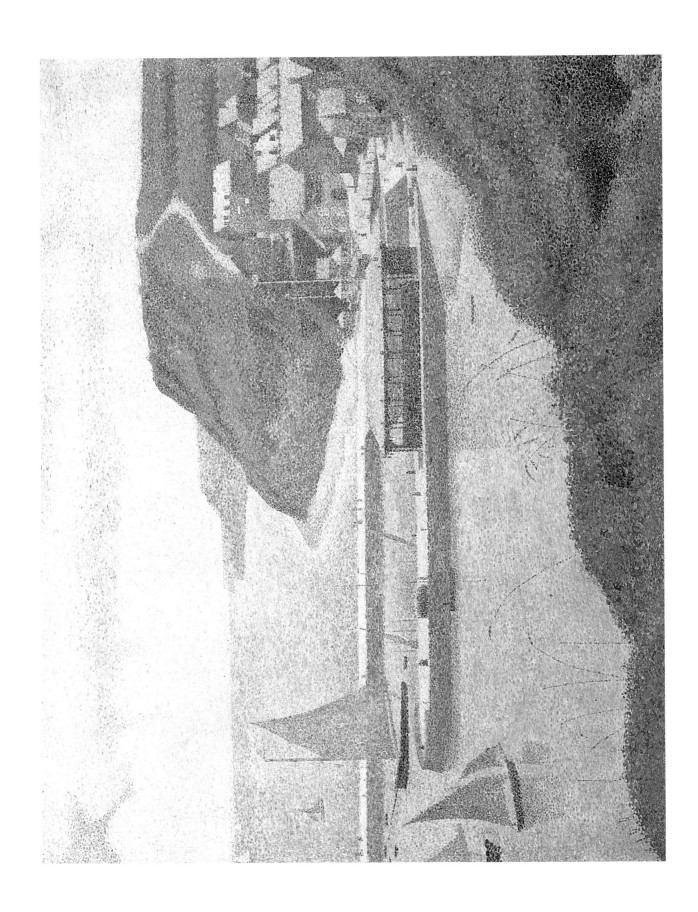

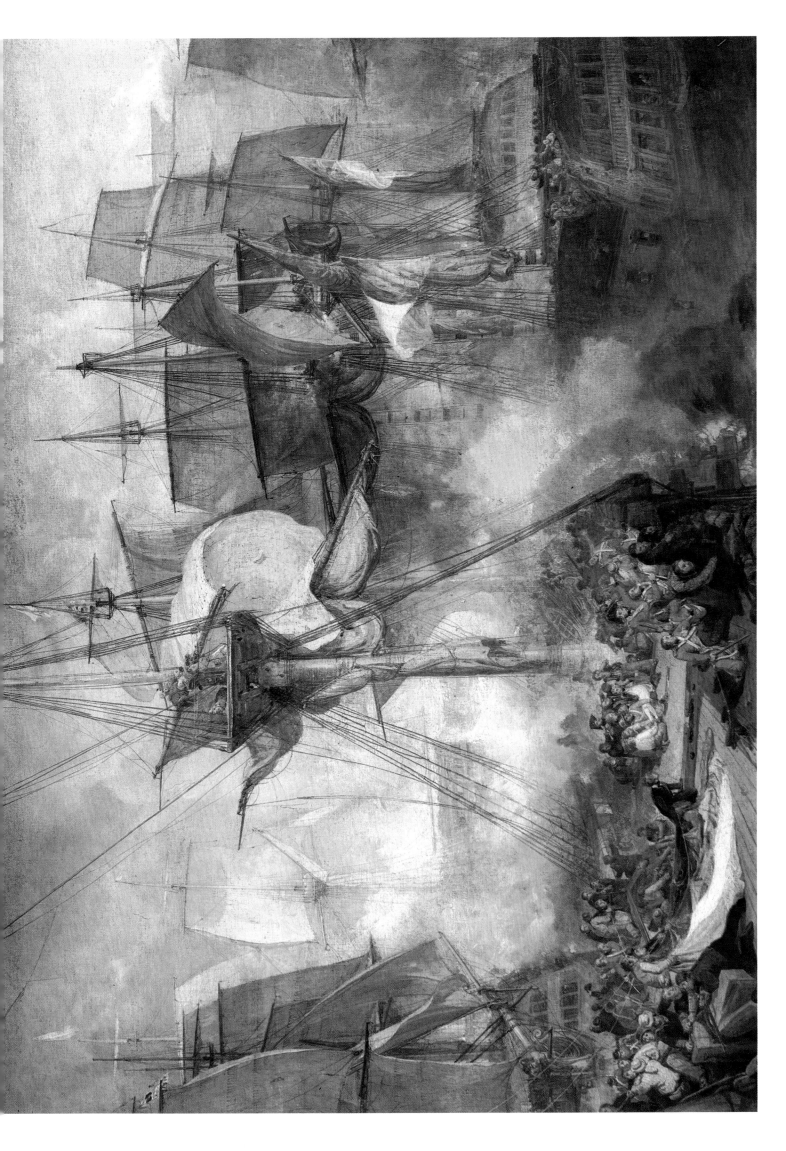